WELCOME TO THE **FAM**

Lessons and activities from our
Female Athlete Mentorship programs,
helping to unlock the **POSSIBLE** in everyone

LANI SILVERSIDES

SG UNITED FOUNDATION
Empowering strong girls for life

WELCOME TO THE FAM

Lessons and activities from our Female Athlete Mentorship programs, helping to unlock the **POSSIBLE** in everyone

LANI SILVERSIDES

SG UNITED FOUNDATION
Empowering strong girls for life

Published by SG United Foundation
PO Box 670
York, ME 03909

hello@sgunitedfoundation.org

"Don't ever underestimate the importance you can have because history has shown us that **courage can be contagious** and hope can take on a life of its own."

~ Michelle Obama

Contents

About SG United Foundation

SG United Foundation ("Strong Girls United") is a nonprofit organization with the mission of **empowering girls and women through sports, mentorship, and mental skills programming**.

We accomplish this through a variety of programs that are led by inspiring female role models, who utilize an evidence-based, trauma-informed curriculum. This curriculum focuses on teaching mental health and mental skills, while also engaging girls and teams in physical activity, sports, and play.

Our motto, "**Strong Bodies, Kind Hearts, Unstoppable Minds**," encapsulates our holistic approach. We thrive at the intersection of multi-sport exposure, fun, social connection, and the sense of belonging that comes from being part of a team. Additionally, we emphasize teaching mental skills and resilience to equip girls with the tools they need to succeed in life.

Learn more at sgunitedfoundation.org or scan the QR code to visit our website and Instagram.

Website:
sgunitedfoundation.org

Instagram:
@stronggirlsunited

"Alone we can do so little; **together we can do so much.**"

- Helen Keller

About the Journal

Female Athlete Mentorship (FAM) goes beyond athletics, embracing a holistic approach with skill-building activities that extend to life lessons. Rooted in the philosophy that **everyone working with girls holds the power to mentor and unlock the POSSIBLE for every girl**, including themselves. our curriculum is a powerful tool for empowering both girls and mentors alike, fostering confidence and resilience.

This journal will take you through our **POSSIBLE themes** and favorite activities. While there are MANY activities related to each theme (many of which can be found in our online FAM activities bank), we have focused on keeping this journal simple and sharing our favorite activities that can be used over and over again. Consider, for example, building them in as habits, like how you brush your teeth every night or buckle your seat belt in a car.

P.O.S.S.I.B.L.E. stands for the eight themes that will be covered in this journal.

Here are some ways this journal is used:

- Our Strong Girls United participants use this journal within our programs which incorporate multiple sports, mentorship, and mental health programming.
- High school and college student-athletes have kept this journal in their bag and used it for their personal journey in sport, whether it be that pre-performance reminder or to build consistent habits strengthening their mental game.
- Trainers, mentors, teachers, and others working 1:1 or with small groups have used this to include mental skills activities into their work.
- Parents have used it with their strong girls - incorporating lessons, routines, and rituals into the dinner table or other parts of home life.

Let's do this!

P.O.S.S.I.B.L.E THEMES

- Practicing Mindfulness
- Overcoming Obstacles
- Setting Goals
- Spreading Kindness
- Investing in Gratitude
- Believing in Yourself
- Leading with Courage
- Embracing a Growth Mindset

Special Acknowledgments

A very special thank you to Sophia Slovenski for her exceptional editing and designing of this journal. Sophia has been a mentor in our FAM program and dedicated two years as an AmeriCorps Up2Us VISTA with our team. As a college athlete herself, she practiced all of these lessons, embodying the principles we cherish. Her enthusiasm and spirit have brought immeasurable value to our organization and the thousands of people it has impacted as a result.

Sophia's design of this journal was guided by our incredible graphic designer since day one, Don Whelan, to whom we owe a great deal of gratitude. His eye and passion for our work as both a graphic designer and as a dad of Strong Girl Lindy has helped move our mission and organization forward.

I also want to extend my heartfelt thanks to the "Chief Strong Girls", Emma and Grace, my daughters who inspired the inception of this organization. Lastly, to my husband Steve, for his diligent editing and unwavering support—thank you.

For more information about our organization and many more activities, you are invited to get involved with Strong Girls United or join our FAM platform at **sgunitedfoundation.org/FAM**

This book is for YOU!

To the strong, kind, and unstoppable girls of the world (that's YOU!)

Remember that you are worthy, beautiful, and capable! Each exercise in this journal is a step towards nurturing a stronger, happier, and more resilient version of yourself. Every effort you put in, no matter how small, practices building the mental skills and resilience. But remember, practice doesn't make perfect. It makes progress. Progress toward finding and expanding our potential and discovering what's possible when we unlock our own inner coach and inner strength.

So, let's dive in and start this journey together. The possibilities are boundless, and the adventure awaits.

You Got This!

MY NAME IS:

THREE THINGS THAT I AM GOOD AT:

MY FAVORITE ACTIVITIES ARE:

WHAT MAKES ME LAUGH:

THREE WORDS THAT DESCRIBE ME:

________ ________ ________

"Don't let anyone define you. **You define yourself!"**

- Billie Jean King

Practicing Mindfulness

Be where your feet are

Learning how to be and live in the present is one of the most powerful things we can do for ourselves. The idea is to recognize when our mind is focused or ruminating on the past or worried about the future. These are both spaces we cannot control. Optimal performance (and well-being) occurs when we are where our feet are – not worried about the final score or a past mistake, but when we are present in the now. We can control our attitudes and responses to this very moment.

Your breath is a great tool to bring yourself back to the present and you and your mentee will practice this each session. Our breath affects every system in our body. It helps us regulate our emotions, decrease stress, calm our nerves, minimize negative thinking. It can reduce our heart rate and help us deal with stressful situations as well as optimize performance.

Whether you are 5 or 55 you can utilize some of these strategies to exercise your "mindfulness muscle".

Activities Include:

- 5 Senses
- Be a STAR
- STOP
- Roller Coaster Breathing
- Coloring

Activity : 5 Senses

Become more present and aware of your surroundings

This activity emphasizes what you are feeling in the moment by using your senses. It can help ground you and bring you to the present moment. Draw or write each of the following:

- **Sight** : 5 things you can see
- **Touch** : 4 things you can feel
- **Hear** : 3 things you can hear
- **Smell** : 2 things you can smell
- **Taste** : 1 thing you can taste

SIGHT

TOUCH

HEAR

SMELL

TASTE

Activity : Be a STAR

S.T.A.R. *stands for* ***Smile · Take a Breath · And · Relax!***

This is a short mindful breathing activity! Think about getting your breath all the way to your belly. And when you "relax" think about dropping your shoulders and unclenching your jaw.

Now draw one of your strengths at each point of the star!

Activity : STOP

S.T.O.P. *stands for* ***Stop · Take a Breath · Observe · Proceed!***

This is a simple mindfulness breathing activity that will help you return to the present moment.

When can you use this? Here are some ideas:

- When I go into the locker room before my game, I will S.T.O.P. (stop, take a breath, observe, and then proceed).
- When I get my assignment in class, I will first S.T.O.P.

Now it's your turn...

When I ______________________________, I will ______________________________

When I ______________________________, I will ______________________________

When I ______________________________, I will ______________________________

When I ______________________________, I will ______________________________

When I ______________________________, I will ______________________________

Activity : Roller Coaster

Inhale and exhale as you trace your fingers

We love practicing roller coasting breathing! In this, you take your pointer finger and trace your other hand. As you go up one side of a finger you breathe in, and as you go down you breathe out.
See the picture below

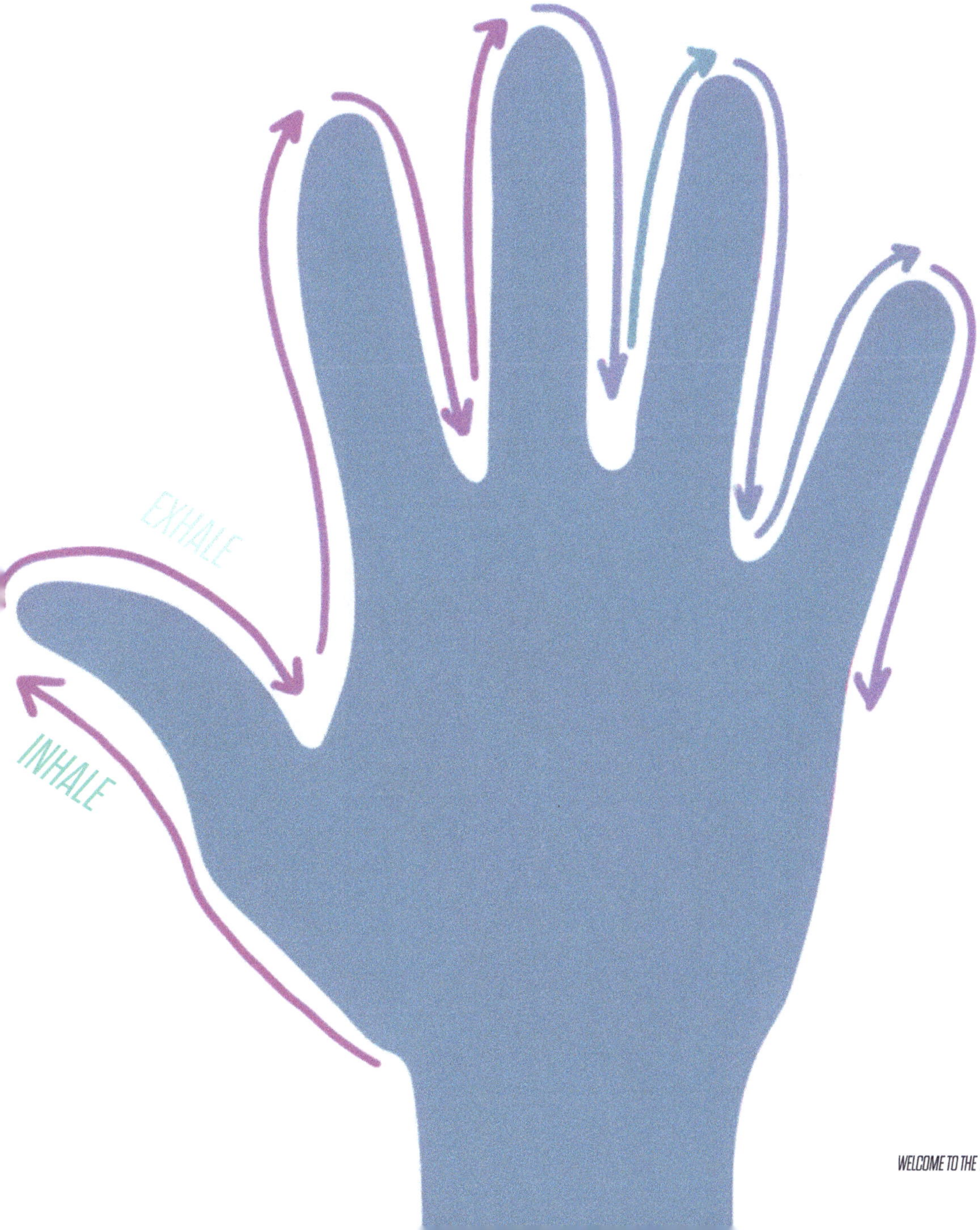

Activity : Coloring

Quiet the mind and tap into your creativity

Let's unplug and unwind. Coloring can sometimes be calming and help you focus on the present moment. Color in the mandala below.

“Practice creates confidence. **Confidence empowers you!**”

- Simone Biles

Overcoming Obstacles

Share your failures

Failure is part of the pathway to success. Self-compassion is a tool that builds mental toughness and resilience. Research tells us that approaching mistakes, failures, and adversities with compassion and encouragement versus self-criticism leads to better relationships and performance, as well as more confidence, motivation, perseverance, and happiness. Mistakes make your brain grow. Science shows it actually grows more when we make mistakes.

"We may encounter many defeats, but we must not be defeated. It may even be necessary to encounter the defeat so that we can know who we are."

-Maya Angelou

Activities Include:

- We're in this together
- Naming Emotions
- How I feel today
- Create your IMR

Activity : We're In This Together

You are not alone.

Sometimes you many run into obstacles or challenges and feel like you are the only person going through a hard time. No matter the circumstances we want you to know that you are not alone and you are loved. In the activity below you will write/draw your support system!

1. Write your name and draw a picture of yourself in the center frame.
2. Write or draw other people around you who support you and whom you feel connected to.
3. Finally, draw a line, bridge, dots, or anything you'd like between you and everyone else to represent the connection you share.

Activity : Naming Emotions

Name it to tame it!

Being able to name emotions helps us understand how we feel, which is key to managing our emotions effectively. It allows us to communicate better with others and build healthy relationships. When we can name our emotions, we're better equipped to navigate life's ups and downs with confidence and resilience.

Color in the emotions you feel today in the wheel below.

You can use this as a tool to come back to and try to name the emotion you are feeling. The further outside you are on the wheel, the more specific you are able to get.

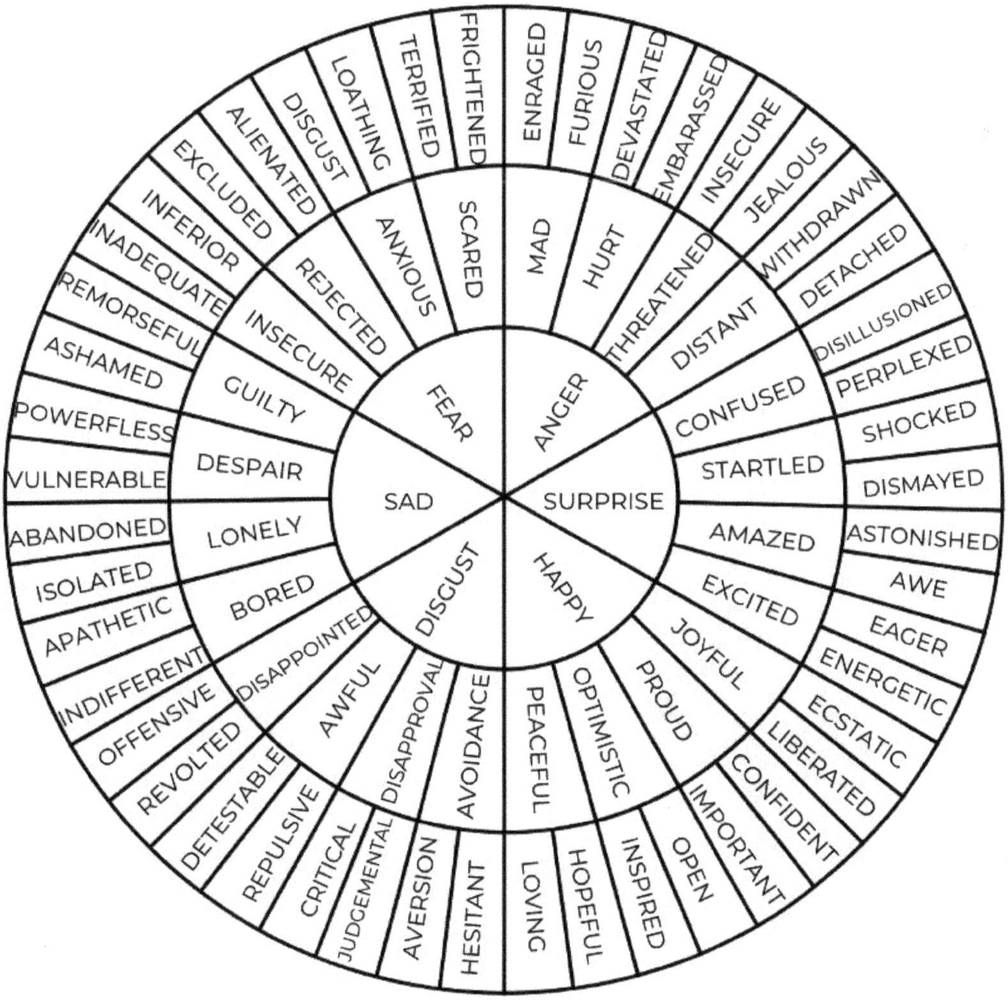

Activity : How I Feel Today

Listen to your body

Draw an arrow on the odometer below to show how your energy levels are feeling today. Then answer the following prompts:

What can I do for myself when/if my tank is low?

What can I do for others when/if my tank is full?

Activity : Creating your IMR

I.M.R. *stands for* ***Individualized Mistake Routine***

This is a great activity for our athletes! Having an IMR can be extremely beneficial, because ALL athletes will make mistakes (even the pros!). Since we know it will happen, let's make a plan for it.

Your ***individualized mistake routine*** can have a combination of a phrase that you can tell yourself and an action you can take to "let it go"!

Here are some example phrases:

- "Next play"
- "Reset"
- "I got this"

Here are some example actions:

- Keep my head up
- Tighten my pony tail
- Fix my shin guard

What's Your IMR?

Phrase:

Action:

"I've never scored a goal in my life without getting a pass from someone else."

- *Abby Wambach*

Spreading Kindness

Create the ripple effect

"Doing an act of kindness produces the single most reliable momentary increase in well-being of any exercise that has been tested." - Dr. Martin Seligman

Kindness practices include doing random acts of kindness and also everyday acts of kindness that do not require money or special skills. Kindness is good for our physical and mental health. Kindness fuels energy, makes you happier, is good for your heart, helps you live longer, increases "feel good" hormones, and more!

"Wherever there is a human being, there is an opportunity for kindness."

-Seneca

Activities Include:

- Kindness counts
- Acts of kindness
- Small joys = Big happiness
- Kindness Quest

Activity : Kindness Counts

The ripple effect in action!

This is a group activity that demonstrates how quickly kind acts can have a ripple effect. Start with your name on the first line and write down 2 names of your peers in the group that you can do a kind act for. Also list something kind you can do.

Now invite those 2 people to name 2 NEW people that they can do a kind act for. And list those actions.

Continue as far as you can. Do you see the ripple effect? It can spread exponentially! If you all continued in this pattern (2 people doing 2 kind acts for 2 new people each time) after 10 days you would have impacted over 1,000 people!

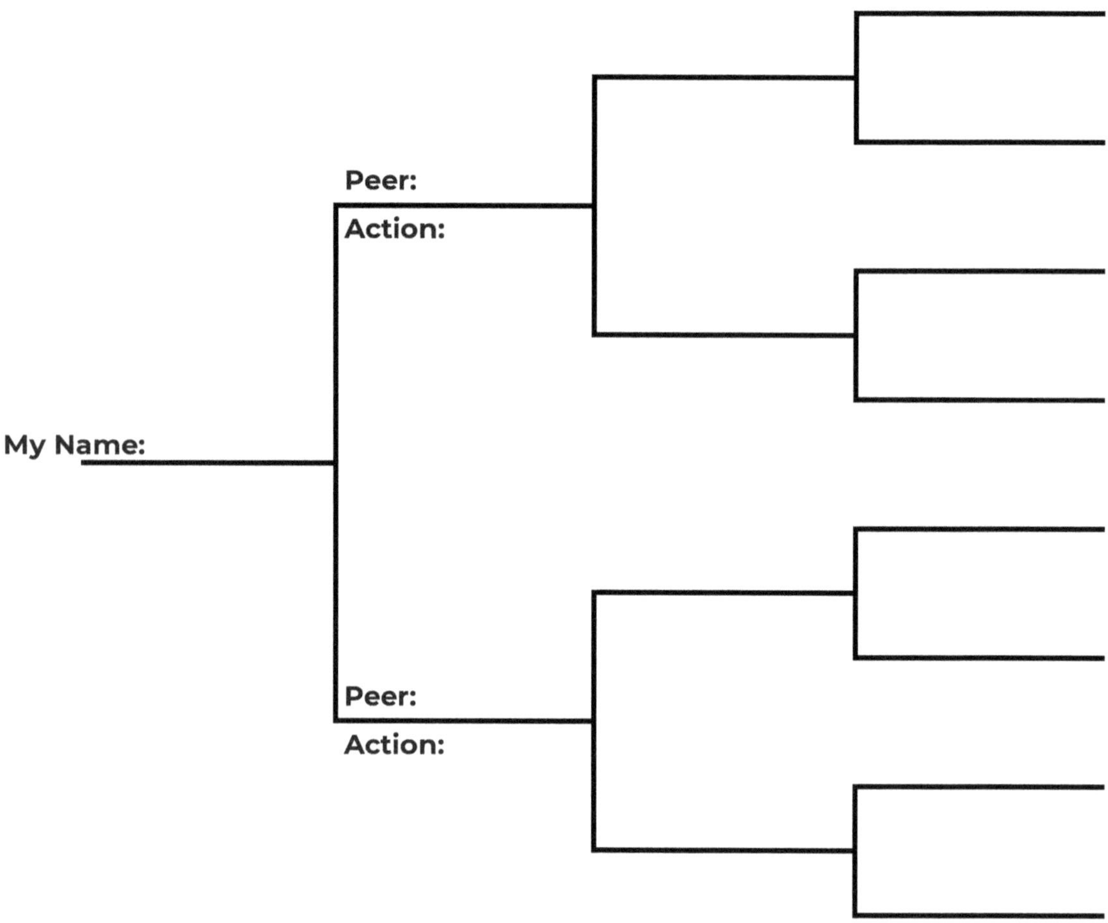

Activity : Acts of Kindness

Positivity and kindness feed off each other

Did you know that being kind can make you a happier person? It's true! Positivity and kindness feed off of each other. In the space below, brainstorm 10 acts of kindness you can do. Be creative and thoughtful in your choices. Consider the needs of others around you. These acts can be as simple as holding the door for someone, sitting with someone new at lunch, or paying someone a compliment.

1.	
2.	
3.	
4.	
5.	
6.	
7.	
8.	
9.	
10.	

Activity : Small Joys = Big Happiness

Choose joy

It's beneficial to notice the small moments in your day-to-day life that bring you joy. Not only does this help you appreciate life more, but it also increases your awareness of the positive impact you can have on others through acts of kindness and your general positivity and awesomeness!

Circle the things that you most identify with as being really awesome:

- Popping bubble wrap.
- High-fiving babies.
- Holiday decorations in public places
- The sound of scissors cutting through construction paper.
- The smell of freshly baked bread
- Peeling an orange in one go.
- Licking the cookie batter off the mixer.
- The first scoop out of a gallon of ice cream.
- Blowing out all the candles of your birthday cake in one shot.
- Free samples of food in the grocery store.
- Air conditioning on a hot day.
- The smell and sound of a campfire.
- Finding money in the couch cushions or pant pockets.
- A baby's laugh.
- Getting that stubborn piece of popcorn out of your teeth.
- Spontaneous dance parties.
- Sneezing multiple times in a row.
- The moment on a roller coaster when you are at the top of the big hill before you go down.
- Walking into fresh snow.
- Sliding on your shoes without having to re-tie them.

Now it's your turn! What are some small but awesome things you notice and can bring a smile or awareness to with your peers?

Activity : Kindness Quest

Let's go on a kindness quest!

Word Search: Find and circle the kindness-related words hidden in the grid below.

Bingo: Find and mark acts of kindness as you complete them. Try to get a full row, column, or diagonal. *(Bonus: Complete the whole board!)*

CARING	POSITIVITY
COMPASSION	RESPECT
COMPLIMENT	SMILE
ENCOURAGE	SPORTSMANSHIP
EMPATHY	SUPPORT
INCLUSION	TEAMWORK
INSPIRE	UPLIFT

J V W F Z P I G I N C L U S I O N Q S P
B R J V R W W H Q E A F V B N A V B Z H
Z C T L K Y I E C E V R W R Z E A O S U
S A T E T R C S C O M P A S S I O N R D
S R R K A E E G L I Z J D X S M I L E U
R I K U S M X S T Z B N J T H E H F R I
Z N I N V P W I P W T G W J B L C Y I [illegible]
F G W Z P B O O Y E P I D I S X O P V D
A M F Y D O D R R X C C Y N Y B M C F S
E S O W E H S L T K W T A S L G P K T I
N W U U D S Y I I S B Y E P P U L A B L
C D R P I L N Z T R M A O I C T I A R U
O W K L P S X U L I K A S R X P M K O B
U A M I E O O P J W V H N E S R E V E L
R P N F X W R V R O B I P S V K N T Q V
A N P T U B T T L Z K M T N H S T U L F
G S X P C R F E N L A H O Y G I F K I K
E S M O E M P A T H Y K T Q Y C P W H I
Q M M V C P A P K I N F X C Q D T D I A
Y J Z D Y M M S P I V O G L J K R U U R

Call a friend	Share a snack with someone	Give someone a high-five	Volunteer (at a local charity, to clean up your neighbor's yard, etc)	Share a positive quote
Compliment yourself in a mirror	Smile at someone	Pick up litter	Write a letter to someone	Tell a friend why you appreciate them
Bake cookies for your neighbors	Talk to someone new today		Say positive-affirmations to yourself	Write about 3 people you are grateful for
Tell a family member you love them	Leave a kind message on a sticky note for someone	Go on a walk with a friend	Clean your bedroom	Write down 3 things you love about yourself
Make gifts or cards for your friends/family	Make someone laugh	Give a genuine compliment	Listen carefully when someone is talking	Call/visit a grandparent or relative

"The only person who can stop you from reaching your goals is **you.**"

- Jackie Joyner-Kersee

Setting Goals

Dream big and start small!

Setting goals regularly and carefully can help you feel in control of your dreams so that you can take the right steps toward making them come true. Setting short-term goals is really fun and can make you feel super accomplished. The kinds of goals in this section are not based on grades, winning, or other results that are out of our control. Goals based on results can make us feel discouraged, whereas goals based on simply completing tasks can make us feel motivated.

"Create the highest, grandest vision possible for your life, because you become what you believe."

-Oprah Winfrey

Activities Include:

- Dream big
- My goals
- Creating your vision

Activity : Dream Big

Dreams are the seeds of inspiration

What is the biggest dream you can possibly imagine?

Some examples may include:

- Being in the Olympics
- Becoming a doctor
- Going into outer space
- Performing on Broadway

No dream is too wild or outrageous!

On the page to the right draw or write your biggest dream! Cut the page out to hang somewhere where you can see it. Some research shows writing down and being able to see, visualize, and share your big dreams can support you on your journey towards them.

Use the space below to brainstorm ↓

Activity : My Goals

What do you aspire to do and be?

This activity prompts you to reflect on various aspects of your life and community, encouraging you to think about what you want to learn, how you can make a positive impact, and what actions you can take to achieve your goals. It's a great way to kickstart your goal-setting process and get motivated to work towards your aspirations.

Answer the following prompts...

- If I could learn about anything, I would like to learn about:

- What I want for the world:

- Here are some ways I can help in my community this year:

- Here are some ways I can be a good friend this year:

- Here are some ways I can help people less fortunate than me:

- Here are some ways I can excel in school:

- To stay physically healthy this year, I will do these 5 things:

Activity : Creating Your Vision

See it to Be it

Mapping out your vision and knowing your values and aspirations can be both fun and incredibly helpful. It allows you to visualize your goals, dreams, and the person you want to become. By creating a vision board, you're able to bring your aspirations to life, inspiring and motivating yourself to take action towards achieving them.

- Start by choosing your **theme word** that goes in the center. This word should encapsulate your main focus or aspiration for the vision board. There are some example words to the right.
- Gather your **materials**. You can use a poster board or a blank piece of paper. Get scissors, glue, markers, and a variety of magazines or printed images and quotes.
- Collect images and words that **inspire** you. Look through magazines and cut out photos, positive messages, and quotes that resonate with your goals and dreams. You can also print images and quotes from the internet if you prefer.
- **Arrange** your items on the board. Place your theme word in the center and arrange the images and quotes around it. Think about how each element relates to your goals and aspirations. Feel free to move things around until you are happy with the layout.
- **Decorate and personalize**. Use markers, stickers, or other decorative elements to add personal touches to your vision board. Write down any additional goals, affirmations, or values that you want to include.
- **Glue** everything in place. Once you are satisfied with the arrangement, glue the images and quotes to the board.
- **Display** your vision board. Place your vision board somewhere you will see it regularly, like your bedroom, office, or another personal space. This will help keep you inspired and focused on your goals.

Remember, your vision board is a personal reflection of your dreams and aspirations, so there is no right or wrong way to create it. Have fun and let your creativity shine!

JOY IMPROVE CREATE FOCUS CALM

BELIEVE BOLD TRUST GROW MINDFUL

“No matter what accomplishments you make, **somebody helps you.**”

- Wilma Rudolph

Investing in Gratitude

Fill your bank account of goodness

Gratitude is a feeling of being thankful and appreciative. You can both feel and show gratitude. Study after study shows that practicing gratitude reduces stress and increases happiness and well-being. Research also shows that gratitude helps you recover quicker from illness or injuries, have better health, exercise more, feel more optimistic, and think more clearly under pressure. Each of these outcomes can have a direct and positive effect on performance and well-being. You can think of gratitude practices as growing your bank account of goodness. You can draw on it during difficult times.

"Gratitude makes what we have, enough."

- Anonymous

Activities Include:

- Three good things
- Gratitude ABCs
- Gratitude jar

Activity : Three Good Things

Train your brain to appreciate the small stuff

This is one of our favorite simple activities that exercises your "gratitude muscle".

What are three good things from your day today:

1.

2.

3.

Now, try this exercise every night for one week!

Example: 1. My oatmeal was delicious this morning. 2. We got to practice relay handoffs at track. 3. I enjoyed listening to music outside today!	**Wednesday:** 1. 2. 3.
Sunday: 1. 2. 3.	**Thursday:** 1. 2. 3.
Monday: 1. 2. 3.	**Friday:** 1. 2. 3.
Tuesday: 1. 2. 3.	**Saturday:** 1. 2. 3.

Activity : Gratitude A. B. C. s

26 reasons you are grateful!

For each letter in the alphabet, fill in something that you are grateful for that begins with that letter:

A. ______________________

B. ______________________

C. ______________________

D. ______________________

E. ______________________

F. ______________________

G. ______________________

H. ______________________

I. ______________________

J. ______________________

K. ______________________

L. ______________________

M. ______________________

N. ______________________

O. ______________________

P. ______________________

Q. ______________________

R. ______________________

S. ______________________

T. ______________________

U. ______________________

V. ______________________

W. ______________________

X. ______________________

Y. ______________________

Z. ______________________

Activity : Gratitude Jar

Your are overflowing with gratitude!

Decorate a jar to have next to your bed with slips of paper. Write down at least one thing each day to add to your jar. When you're feeling really down one day, open the jar and read the slips of paper to help bring you back up! To get you thinking, you can fill in this jar with answers to some of these prompts:

- I'm grateful for these people in my life:
- I'm grateful for these activities:
- I'm grateful for these books:
- I'm grateful for these movies:
- I'm grateful for these foods:
- I'm grateful for these songs:
- I'm grateful for these weather conditions:
- I'm grateful for these moments in history:
- I'm grateful for these skills I have:
- I'm grateful for these places:

Activity : Gratitude Tree

Plant seeds of gratitude and watch them grow

Add leaves to the tree below and in each leaf write something that you are thankful for.

When dealing with disappointment, acknowledge your feelings and then think of the good things in your life. Coming back to this tree might help you!

"When the whole world is silent, even **one voice becomes powerful.**"

- Malala Yousafzai

Believing in Yourself

Practice thinking confidently

Confidence is a belief in your own abilities and qualities. Developing your confidence helps you try new things, cope with challenges and mistakes, and take pride in who you are and your accomplishments. Confidence can come as a result of how you think and what you focus on. Confidence isn't determined by how you feel, but rather how you think. And if it's a thought, then you are in charge of it! Confidence is boosted with power poses, self-talk, self-affirmations, exercise (sweating!), and smiling! We aim to teach how to think confidently and have the power over it.

"Don't let anyone define you. You define yourself."
- Billie Jean King

Activities Include:

- I AM...
- Power pose
- Go to statement
- Modeling heroes

Activity : I AM...

Strong, Kind, Unstoppable!

Affirmations are positive statements that you say to yourself to encourage and support a positive mindset. They help you focus on your strengths and build confidence.

Write at least three affirmations on the poster on the next page. Cut out and decorate the poster, then hang it in your room or somewhere you can see it every day! Affirmations are positive statements like “I am strong,” “I am confident,” and “I am unique,” rather than specific roles like “I am a basketball player.”

Brainstorm ideas below ↓ ↓ ↓

I AM

Activity : Power Pose

"Our bodies change our minds, our minds change our behaviors, and behavior changes outcomes." ~ *Amy Cuddy*

A power pose is a pose that displays confidence and strength. Power poses have been shown to increase confidence and decrease stress . A typical power pose entails standing up straight and pulling your shoulders back.

Here are some power poses for you to try:

Don't like any of these poses? Make up your own!
Draw your power pose in the space below:

Activity : Go to statement

Build yourself up

Before a test in school, a game, or a new activity, it can be helpful to have a go-to statement. A go-to statement is a statement that's prepared ahead of time so that in a challenging moment, you have something you can say to yourself to give you the confidence boost you need. These statements can be really simple! **"I got this!"** or **"I am ready for this"** often do the trick.

Write down three go-to statements in the space below. If you are having trouble creating your statement, think of what your parents or coach might say when they're giving you a pep talk.

1

2

3

Activity : Modeling Heroes

Who do you look up to?

One effective way to build confidence is to mirror and model your heroes. Think about someone you admire greatly. How do they act? What habits do they have? How can you learn from them? By understanding and emulating the qualities and behaviors of your heroes, you can develop similar traits in yourself and boost your confidence.

Answer the questions below...

- Who is someone you look up to and admire? This could be a family member, a famous person, a teacher, or a friend.

- How do they act?

- What routines and habits do you think they have that help them?

- What is one specific action or habit from your hero that you will start practicing this week?

Activity : Design Your Dream Jersey

Wear your confidence proudly!

Color and create your own unique sports jersey. Be sure to add your name and number.

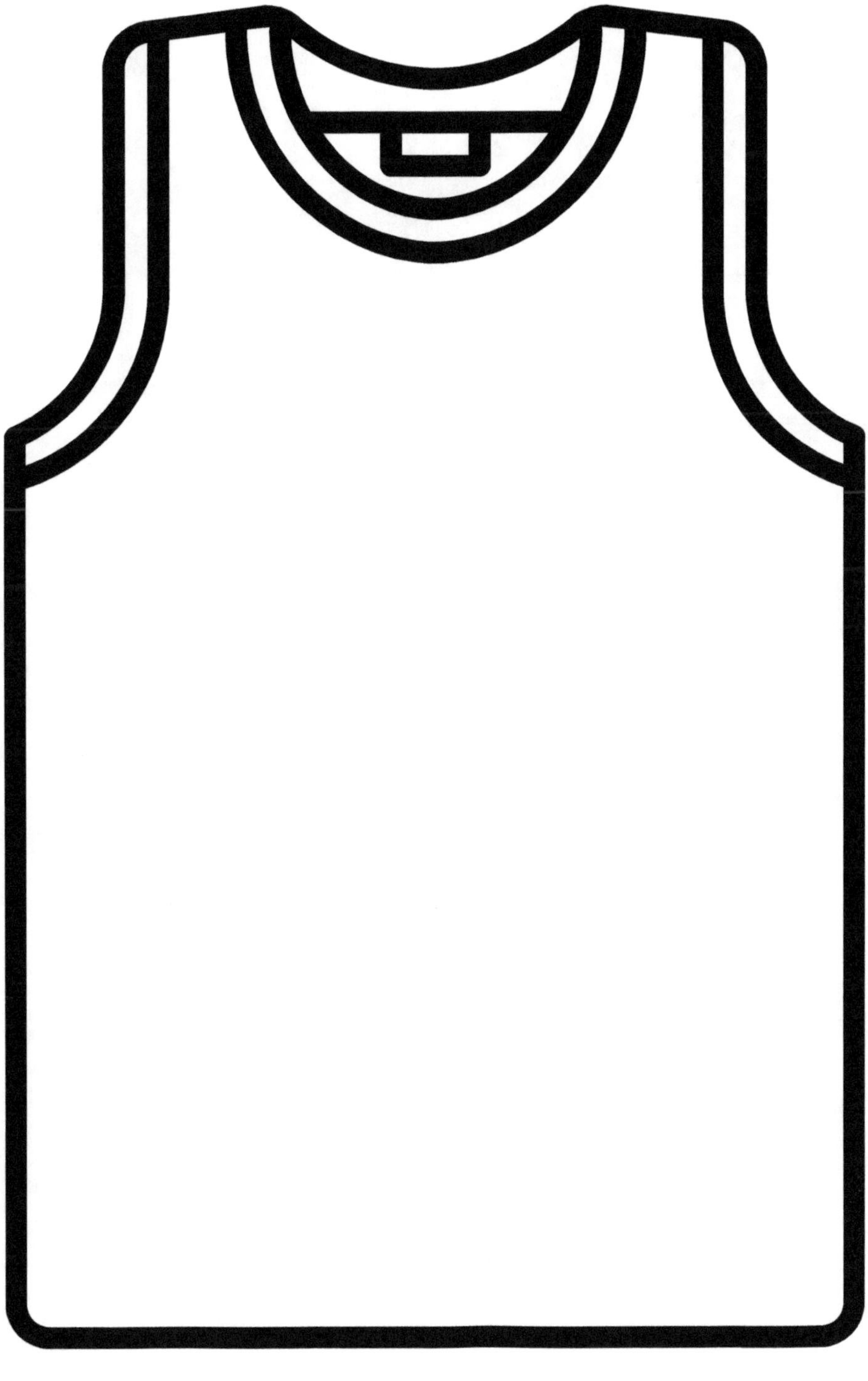

“Every woman's success should be an inspiration to another. **We're strongest when we cheer each other on.**”

- Serena Williams

Leading with Courage

Taking brave action

Oftentimes people think being courageous or brave means that they are not afraid. But being afraid, nervous, fearful, or scared is totally normal, especially when it comes to standing up for something, trying a new activity, or doing what's right. Having courage just means that you still do all those things in spite of being afraid. It means that the fear is still there, but it doesn't control you. This is really important because girls get messages to be "fearless." Fear is normal and you can take brave actions. Each time you take a brave action or do something outside of your comfort zone, you are growing this bravery muscle. And being a leader takes courage. We want you to aim to be brave over perfect

"People who are truly strong lift others up. People who are truly powerful bring others together."

-Michele Obama

Activities Include:

- Your strengths
- Butterflies
- Being your authentic self
- Great leaders make mistakes

Activity : Your Strengths

You have so many strengths!

Use the list below to help you identify and recognize your unique strengths . By reflecting on your abilities, you'll gain confidence to lead with courage. Circle all the strengths you associate with, then write your top 5 below and answer the follow-up questions.

- Adaptable
- Coachable
- Collaborative
- Committed
- Compassionate
- Confident
- Creative
- Determined
- Disciplined
- Empathetic
- Focused
- Hardworking
- Honest
- Independent
- Intelligent
- Kind
- Motivated
- Organized
- Positive
- Resilient
- Resourceful
- Responsible
- Self-disciplined
- Supportive

Write your own:

- ___________
- ___________

My Top 5 Strengths:

1.
2.
3.
4.
5.

Which strengths are you most proud of?

What are three strengths you are actively working on? And how?

How can you use one of these strengths to lead with courage in the future?

Activity : Butterflies

Let the butterflies fly!

Your body may experience stress or nerves in different ways. You might have butterflies in your stomach or you might feel your heart pounding. Your breath may feel different, such as being short and shallow. Here is the thing – how you think about these physiological responses matters and can transform your experience with them!

Rather than trying to push away the butterflies or the uncomfortable feelings, you can choose to welcome them. You do this by thinking and knowing that this is simply your body preparing you to meet a challenge. Whenever you feel butterflies in your stomach, think about letting the butterflies fly, and know that this is your body is giving you courage to move forward.

In the butterflies, write down some things that make you feel stress or nervousness.

Now let these butterflies FLY! In the space below write a statement you can use every time you feel this way, such as "This is the way champions feel" or "Let the butterflies fly" or "This is how my body prepares me to perform" or "I can do hard things"!

Activity : Being Your Authentic Self

You are meant to stand out!

Fill in the mirror with answers to the following prompts:

5 things I love about myself...

My friends think I'm awesome because...

I feel happy when I...

I'm really proud of...

I mean a lot to ...

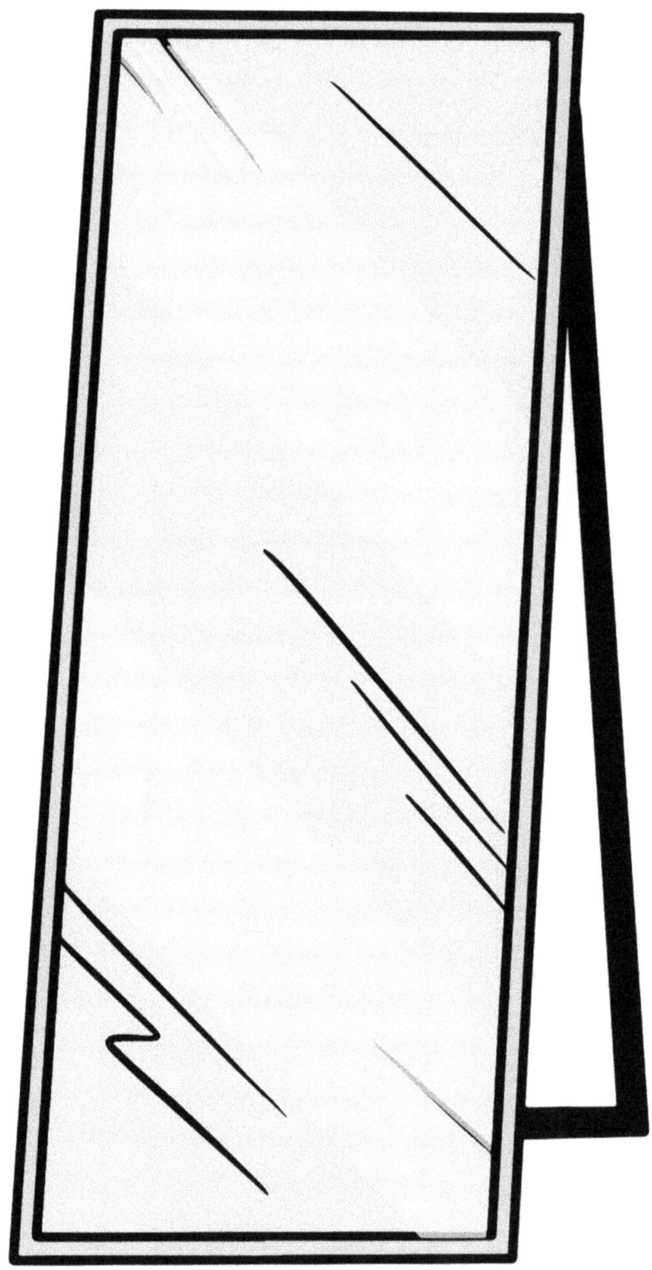

Activity : Great Leaders Make Mistakes

Everybody makes mistakes

Leaders are not perfect! But they do learn from their mistakes. Leaders might follow these steps when making a mistake.

1. Own the mistake
2. Forgive themselves (self-compassion!)
3. Learn from their mistake
4. Make a plan so the same mistake doesn't happen again
5. Keep trying new things—even if mistakes could happen!

Think of a time that you made a mistake and fill in the blanks below ↓

One time, I ____, but I forgive myself.

From my mistake, I learned that ____.

Next time, to avoid making this mistake, I'll be sure to ______________________________.

I'm still a strong and capable person. Onward!

"I really think a champion is defined not by their wins but by how they can recover when they fall."

-SERENA WILLIAMS

“We may encounter many defeats but **we must not be defeated.**”

- Maya Angelou

Embracing a Growth Mindset

The power of YET!

Our mindset can be thought of as our attitude toward and outlook on life. It has been studied and shown that there are two types of mindsets: a growth mindset and a fixed mindset. In a fixed mindset, people believe their ability, talent, and intelligences are "fixed" traits that cannot be changed. You either have it or you don't! (You are either smart or you're not! You are either talented or you're not!)

On the other hand, a growth mindset is the belief that your ability, talent, and intelligence can grow and be developed through hard work and consistent effort. Having a growth mindset is an important step to becoming your strongest and happiest self! A growth mindset allows you to embrace feedback and new opportunities, and also to take on challenges and face mistakes.

One of the most powerful things you can do is add the word "yet" to the end of any sentence that starts with, "I can't."

Activities Include:

- Trying something new
- . . . YET
- Controlling controllables
- Who am I?

Activity : Trying Something New

Step out of your comfort zone

Trying new things can be a powerful way to build a growth mindset and boost your confidence. When you step out of your comfort zone, you learn more about yourself, discover new interests, and realize that you are capable of more than you thought. Every new experience, whether successful or not, helps you grow and become more resilient.

Let's make a plan to try some new things using the prompts below!

Write down 3 new foods or recipes you want to try:

Write down 3 new artists/genres you want to try listening to:

Write down 3 new books or poems you want to read:

Write down 3 new things you want to try this week:

Activity : . . . YET!

Changing your mindset

Finding ways to add to your self-talk the idea that growth is possible and perfection is not the goal is important. We are going to give you some ideas. Fill in the blanks below with your own experiences.

I'm not the best at ____________________ but with practice, I can improve.

I'm not confident about ________________________ but with persistence, I'll grow.

I'm not comfortable with _______________________ but the more I do it, the easier it will get.

I'm not excited about _________________________ but I will have an open mind about it, and it will be okay.

One word that can change your attitude is **...YET**! This word leaves room for growth and improvement. Fill in the following sentences and then add **YET** to the end of every sentence.

"I'm not good at ____ ____ ____ ____."

"I am unable to do ____ ____ ____ ____."

"I tried ____ but it didn't work ____ ____ ____."

Hear a friend say they can't do something? Add YET to the end of their sentence for them to encourage them to keep trying!

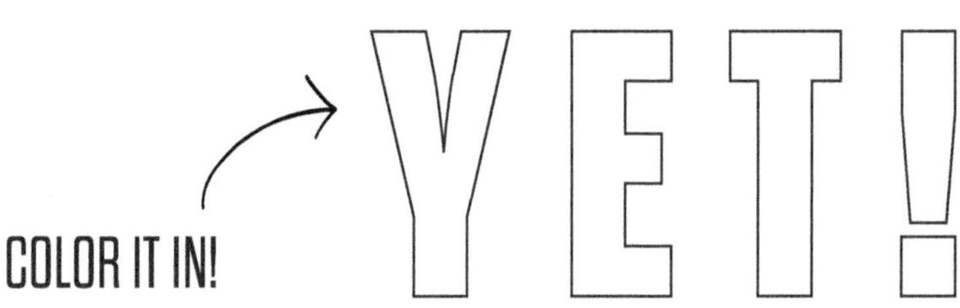

Activity : Controlling Controllables

Focus on what you have power over!

Understanding what is within our control and what is not is essential for maintaining a healthy mindset and managing stress effectively. By focusing our energy on the things we can control, we can influence outcomes and take proactive steps towards our goals. And being able to try not to focus too much on the things we can't control can help us keep a growth mindset.

Place the phrases below into the correct place in the diagram. The things we can control should go INSIDE of the human shape. The things we can't control should go on the OUTSIDE. **Add more phrases of your own to each section!**

- The weather
- Traffic
- What other people say or do
- My actions
- My behavior
- My outlook
- My words
- How tall I am
- Coach decisions
- Who my friends are

Activity : Who Am I?

"Knowing yourself is the beginning of all wisdom" *- Aristotle*

Take some time to reflect on the questions below then write your answers in the space available. There are no right or wrong answers only answers that are true to you!

Questions	Your Answers
What core values guide you?	
What are your future goals?	
Who or what inspires you?	
What are you grateful for?	
How do you want to grow?	
What challenges have you overcome?	
What positive affirmations/quotes motivate you?	
What are your biggest dreams?	
What does a healthy lifestyle look like for you?	
What adventures or fun experiences do you want to have?	

HUDDLE UP

Make Your Game Plans

You've put in the work, explored new mental skills, and learned strategies to strengthen your mindset. Now, it's time to make a game plan for how you'll keep practicing!

Think about:

- Your favorite activities from this book—what worked best for you?
- How you can use these skills in daily life, school, and sports.

Use the pages that follow to write out your game plan! Consider these prompts:

- Gratitude: What's your favorite gratitude practice? Can you plan to share good things every night at dinner?
- Mindfulness & Breathing: When will you use a new breathing or mindfulness technique to stay focused?
- Affirmations: What are your top three affirmations to boost confidence?
- Teamwork & Connection: How will you support and uplift your teammates?

Reflect and write down some plans!

A Note to Athletes

Dear Athlete,

As you close this journal, I want you to remember something crucial: **You are not defined by your performance**. Whether it's on the field, in the classroom, or in any aspect of your life, your worth extends far beyond numbers and scores. Embrace your uniqueness, for it is what makes you truly extraordinary. As you continue your journey, remember that building mental strength is just as important as physical prowess. Cultivate confidence, resilience, mindfulness, and goal-setting skills as if they are muscles you can work on and strengthen. You will then be able to serve as your inner coach, guiding you through challenges and victories alike. We don't strive for perfection; we strive to discover our potential and what's possible! So dream big while also remembering to celebrate the small awesome things too.

We are with you with unwavering support!

YOU ARE PART OF OUR **FAM**

Signing off with
STRONG BODIES. KIND HEARTS. UNSTOPPABLE MINDS.

Lani Silversides
Mental Performance Coach
Founder and Executive Director of SG United Foundation

A Note to Coaches

Dear Coach,

Congratulations on choosing to incorporate this journal into your coaching regimen. By doing so, you're not only focusing on the physical aspects of training but also recognizing the importance of mental strength in the development of your athletes. By teaching these skills, you're empowering your athletes to navigate challenges both on and off the field.

I understand the immense dedication and countless hours you invest in coaching, both on and off the field. Your commitment goes beyond the scheduled practices and games; it's the countless hidden hours spent thinking about how to best support your athletes and team.

And for female sports, in particular, you are an integral part of your athletes' lives, providing guidance, support, and mentorship during a critical stage of their development. We know:

- Participation in sports and physical activity has been shown to support long-term health, achievement, and well-being.
- Female high school athletes are 41% more likely to graduate from college within six years compared to those who did not participate in sports.
- Girls who engage in athletics often report greater contentment with their lives, higher self-esteem, and lower levels of depression.
- 1 in 3 people grow up without a mentor

Remember, as you support your athletes, it's crucial to prioritize your own well-being too. Just as you encourage your team to build mental strength, resilience, and mindfulness, remember to apply these principles to your own life. Take care of yourself, both physically and mentally, so you can continue to be the supportive mentor your athletes need.

Thank you for your dedication to the growth and well-being of your athletes.

Signing off with
STRONG BODIES. KIND HEARTS. UNSTOPPABLE MINDS.

Lani Silversides
Mental Performance Coach
Founder and Executive Director of SG United Foundation

A Note to Parents

Dear Parents,

As you embark on this journey with your daughters in sports, I want to extend my gratitude for your support and commitment. By getting this journal, you are supporting our nonprofit organization while also nurturing growth, both on and off the field. I'm excited to share with you how you can utilize this journal to further support your girls and strengthen your family bond.

I encourage you to consider integrating the activities in this journal into your family's daily routine. You can choose one or two exercises and make them a part of your everyday life. For example, you can try the "three good things" gratitude activity every night at dinner, where each family member shares three "good" things from their day. Or, you can incorporate the mindfulness STAR activity into your morning routine as you head out the door, reminding each other to be a STAR (Stop, Take a Breath, And Relax).

Additionally, I encourage you to expose your daughters to women's sports by attending local high school or college games. Female athletes serve as powerful role models, inspiring girls to pursue their athletic passions and empowering them to believe in their own potential. We know exposure to strong female role models helps both get girls in the game and keep them in the game.

Even if sports or athletics isn't your child's passion, these activities to build mental strength and resilience are valuable in any pursuit they choose. Whether it's music, art, academics, or any other interest, the skills they develop through these exercises will serve them well in all aspects of their lives.

Thank you for being champions of your girls (and our) dreams and aspirations!

Signing off with
STRONG BODIES. KIND HEARTS. UNSTOPPABLE MINDS.

Lani Silversides
Mental Performance Coach
Founder and Executive Director of SG United Foundation

JOIN THE FAM

Did you enjoy this book? Want more inspiring material? **JOIN THE FAM!**

FAM *stands for* ***Female Athlete Mentorship***
A Comprehensive Platform, Curriculum, Movement, and Community for Those Working With Girls from Kindergarten to College

At STRONG GIRLS UNITED, we believe in the transformative power of mentorship and the development of mental skills through sports, empowering individuals to excel both on and off the field.

Discover the Pillars of FAM & Our P.O.S.S.I.B.L.E. Curriculum
Female Athlete Mentorship (FAM) goes beyond athletics, embracing a holistic approach with skill-building activities that translate into valuable life lessons. Our curriculum is designed to empower girls and mentors alike, fostering confidence, resilience, and personal growth. Everyone working with girls has the potential to mentor and unlock the POSSIBLE for every girl, including themselves.

Unlock Over Four Years of Content and Activities
Our new FAM platform and community are here to support you with research-backed programs and ideas. Whether you're bringing these initiatives to your community or starting your own local project, we've got you covered!

Learn more/sign up today:

www.sgunitedfoundation.org/fam

www.ingramcontent.com/pod-product-compliance
Lightning Source LLC
La Vergne TN
LVHW070857210926
848482LV00016B/958